MY SOBER LITTLE MOON

BY:
JON LUPIN, THE POETRY BANDIT

My dearest Julie,
You know this song and dance,
but I hope you find it moving still.

Much love

ISBN-13: 978-1717170934
ISBN-10: 1717170935
First Print Edition: 2016
Second Print Edition: 2018

For the Newcomer,
or that person coming back,
for those seeking self control,
and healing through creativity,
this is for you.

Inkling

I could never find ink dark enough to blot out the memory
of my first drunk:

I swam to the darkest part of the ocean, a place where only
the fleeting dreams of the boastful dance upon the surface,
like shiny fish, looking for a home in the sky, as if the water
were a prison. When those dreams were too thick to think
around, I would dive down until my head would feel a
pressure so distinct it felt like it had always been a part of
my life.

It was suffocating, and intoxicating, and I needed to go
deeper, every time. It drove me mad.

Was there a way out?
A voice reverberated in the dense fog of my mind:
Ink. I needed Ink.

I knew, in the depths, I would find her.
Leviathan.

She knew I was coming for her ink. I figured if she gave it
up freely, it would never be dark enough, black enough …
so a fight is how it had to be.

Every day, I would lose and she would swim away easily,
leaving me to lick my wounds and remember the taste of
china whites on my nineteenth birthday. It stung, sour like
bile in the throat, it gave me indigestion, much like every lie
afterward.

This is why I came back to her, wrestling for that one thing
I believed would set me free:

Ink; I needed Ink. And I knew, without it, I would die.

Frolicking Heretic

Wine was a lover
not fit for me and
not fit for sharing;
I took her anyway,
to all the fancy affairs,
frantic and fantastic,
full of frolic and heretic,
she gave me a permit,
broke me and
made me a hermit.
She left me gutted
in the gutter,
fancy no longer;
I swore she had the last laugh.
I took her anyway,
bought her what she wanted,
and drank with her again the next day.

The Early Years

The pedestal was a bad place for us,
and though we built it from the stone and mortar,
chipped and cut from our early years of love,
it never seemed strong enough to hold the weight
of the baggage we brought along to the top.
So, with contraption and understatement,
hooking and rigging,
snip-snapping and reconditioning
the way we think and move and have our being,
we turned that pedestal into an altar
and sacrificed that baggage
in hopes a second chance
would bring back the mystery
we had in those early years of commitment.

C h o r u s

The nightingales
never gave us a chance
to join in the chorus,
so we burned up our verses
in a night of bad drinks
and poor choices.

My Esau

Oh, and I can see it in your eyes,
that hoarding of strength for just one last time to hit the
town with everything we got, and trust me, nothing within
me or without would stop me from doing just that. I would
throw it all away for just one more crazy night of your
stupid favorite fruity drinks and terrible music choices;
peeing in front of Parliament, paying people to roll down
their windows to receive our half eaten hot dogs, and
creeping back in hoping no one cared, but I sense you are
ready to give up on anything like this happening again. We
both know that this cannot happen, for her sake, for their
sake, or for mine. We grew together! An Esau rolled in the
gore of redness and hating second-best, cursing God for
making you last, and a Jacob always thinking of himself,
thinking he could best the Angels and too afraid to climb
his own ladder to the top and see what all the fuss is
about.

As different as we might be, the same fighting chances we
both had are our lessons learned.

Hang on to those handfuls of flesh written with the
accolades I gave you much too late in this life; I always
was a prick but now I realize I need you, my Esau; don't
leave me to climb that ladder later in life alone.

My Sober Little Moon

It's happening again -
that overflowing of cups,
that "no control" "out of control,"
that dizzy devilish declaration of destruction.

I guess I deserve it for laying it out on the table like a
bouquet of gas station "I'm sorry's" that died in the car
while I was circling the block figuring out how to explain the
booze on my slithering tongue.

But she loved me, truly loved me, more than any other,
so while I became happy with becoming
friends with the hum of the furnace in her heart,
nothing felt better than her first words spoken in
forgiveness.

So contrary to what you've heard, I do love wolves and
cats and Roses most of all,
but all I need right now is the friendly hand of a stranger
to wipe my tears away
and call evens
and damn the odds like a left-handed kid in boarding
school.

So beat me, bind me, berate me, break me,
but never believe that I will hate you in return,
because I have seen the kind face of forgiveness
on this dark side of my sober little moon.

My Sober Little Moon by: Jon Lupin, The Poetry Bandit

My Sober Little Moon by: Jon Lupin, The Poetry Bandit

Gnarled Knuckles

I can never win that war,
where my defense begins with the
sound of my own bones
stressing and crackling,
like a kindling puppet burning quickly
in a fire I set myself
the night before with a bottle of red wine
and a couch soaked in alcoholic sweat.

But I have learned since,
there is
something greater than myself
worth fighting against
and that is
the thought of my children
hearing the hiss and pop of those
wooden puppet limbs and
thinking I've given up,
so until then,
I bare my
knotted, gnarled knuckles
and fight this demon until I'm ready
to tell them why their daddy
doesn't drink at dinner.

Uneven

Uneven bedsheets,
coffee without milk,
burlap for comfort,
gravel is silk,
little spiders play
hide and go seek
between the hairs of my body
until I fall asleep.
Meet the humans by day
and the demons at night.
When you wake, you pray
to see some kind of light.
And when the meetings are done,
all that lingers for me
are the tempting stares
and fire-licking tongues.

Gems

Every word and every pause,
every gaze not met
ripped open my chest,
allowing you to run that bony finger
up and down my ribcage
looking for them,
those three little gems.
I hid them from you
because they were all I had
and I was saving them
for somebody else.

Little Red

Lately,
I've been so doggone tired,
and when I say "tired" I don't mean
I'm strung out on my daybed,
forlorn and begging the sandman to
beat me senseless –
no, I'm tired
as in, I'm tired of always carrying this desire around
like Red carried Hell in a handbasket to
Grandmother.
She may have loved her enough to bring
some stale baking,
but she brought the wolf, too …
and that is how I feel.

I carry my secret napalm dreams
of drinking everywhere I go,
gassing the whole lot of
family and friends along the merry way, but
that is how it is when you are in recovery:
with the best of intentions,
I bring the wolf
in a bloody gas mask.

Tainted Hippie Corn

Can you see this malaise?
It creeps into our souls like molasses matted
with mysterious messages,
making you feel like you've eaten too much,
drank too much, smoked too much,
munch, munch munch,
less is more and more is not enough.
I'm not one for conspiracy theories
or secret guilds guiding our moral compasses
with tainted hippie corn or
hidden treasuries on the back of my
fruity candied gluten-free cereal,
but what I do know
is that
we are all out to get ourselves.

We're just waiting for that bag
to slip over our heads,
for that plunge into the icy cold water
in a trough,
in a barn somewhere in the country,
where no one
can hear our screams.

This might sound like a giving up
or more of a giving in,
but melancholy can be fleeting
and maybe that's why I think it's okay
to drift away into a
sweet conspiracy theory
about myself once in a while.

Humidity

We held sparklers
on a humid summer's night
and watched
as our love fizzled out
one more time.

Darklings

In the Deep,
that part of my heart closed off
to friends and family,
is where my Darklings play.
In the sludge of my despair
I could not have faired
any better
than a lame mare
in a race it was never meant to care about.
And so they play with my attenuated soul
and weigh it down,
keeping it from knowing that the race
was meant to be won.

All I know is that when the dust settles,
I will be free from my Darklings
and no longer have to move in slow motion.

In this Bed

At night,
I sleep stiffly
like a dead man in full rigor,
afraid I might turn over
during my slumber
and fall into this maddening
emptiness you've left behind
in this bed.

Red Rum

Some are made of ash and bone,
while some of them will walk alone.
Some will return and some will expire,
while others burn, some play the crier,
"To the Point with Jaguar's fang!"
They glint and gleam,
a forest gang,
and live their lives as if nothing
could choke them.
But the rest of us who do not fly
choose a path with little light,
but always find that when it's dim
we see the best things come from Him.
So murder me, or murder light;
murder crows, or say goodnight;
the path you've chosen will define
if you'll bathe in smooth blood wine.

Vineyards

Stuck between two paces of living,
we fight for the front line,
the chance to be heard and to be seen.
The finish line will get further away
if we get further from each other,
leaving us wandering
without cover.
So,
hold my hand; stand with me.
Let's walk together,
not with the others.
What do they know anyway?
We grew a vineyard,
they only grew weeds.

At Sea

Everyone wants to know
but I can't say,
and even if I did,
what good is another sunken ship?
You see, that's the thing about forgiveness.
You can't go back
and if you did,
like a dog to his vomit
or swine wearing pearls
found in the folds of their muddy skin,
that would be your burden to bear.
But if you want to sink ships,
pop a pill and go to sleep,
because in your dreams
is the safest place
to execute men at sea.

Serenade

When sadness serenades her softly,
she selects him as her muse.
Madness meets her maliciously,
making claims of love,
caressing her tightly.
Back and forth they jockey,
neither wants to lose
that special place in the
hot, damp air,
where she chooses between
Stark and Light.

From Father

Go forth with your eyes gouged out and
your soul bitten by the serpent;
bleed a little,
suffer want,
stand a while on broken feet,
with a congealing spirit,
lay forever on a bed of
broken springs.
Your life has just begun;
it will be hard, but love will come.
And when it does,
do not let it go, my son.

The Bear

My child, I'm tired of running from you and
I worry, one day, that you'll see it, too,
the madness within has replaced my muse.
So go tell your Father and get him his gun,
I'm tired of fighting, I'm setting my sun.
Cry if you must, I know that it hurts,
but listen up close, and listen with care,
I'll live in the stars as long as you stare,
for no one can kill
the soul of The Bear.

My Sober Little Moon by: Jon Lupin, The Poetry Bandit

The Hum

It was never about the way she brushed her hair,
or how she smiled when she dressed,
and
it wasn't even about the way she took my breath away
when she laughed.
No, it was the wonderment
when she stood alone,
eyes closed,
no pain,
no sequence,
no numbers,
no pen and no paper,
just her in the silence,
dancing to the hum
of the machine
of her imagination.

My Sober Little Moon by: Jon Lupin, The Poetry Bandit

Jilted

Jilted lovers
hiding under quilted covers
lie and cheat, steal the sweet;
it's only about the thrill.
So when that bell rings
and the caged bird sings,
she will take her leave –
he will beg reprieve!
Short and sweet,
ruined tearful sleeves,
lovesick, can't eat,
he bit her bullet
and lost this game of
roulette.

Burning Man

When his flame
catches up to my name,
will I be tired enough
to let it engulf
all that I am and
all that I've done?
Or will I be allowed
to wander hallowed halls,
afraid that I might falter
and end up lying on that altar?

Either way, I'm destined to be a burning man.

Imperfect

I can see that it's killing you; you want to turn to the last
page in my story just to see the look on my face when you
tell me you weren't lying, that you meant it when you said
this would all come crashing down upon my house, like a
diseased oak, tired from the battering rams of the wind.
Well, go ahead, turn ahead. You'll miss all the good parts
in between. As for the ending, well, you see that is how I've
changed. I have no interest in knowing how it ends for me.
I've let that go, but if you want to follow me through the
story, take off your white sheet, your coward's cloak and
put on some rubber boots, because it's going to get messy.
Nothing is perfect, and it was never supposed to be.
Ghosts can't pray anyway, so please stay with me; just
shut up and hold my hand.

Futurism

The future is a woman
dressed in robes flowing with the
blood of poets who wrote about her
too late in life.
She is attended to by cherubs with wrists
chained to cases
full of pills and dirty things,
waiting to be handed off to the highest
bidder on a street darker than
Hell could muster.

Her voice carries across memories,
and she scatters doubt
to the four corners of the globe
because she is wanting,
and she is needy.

She is a leech who never stops
fawning over the
fact she will never know
true love.

Nobody is in love with the future
except those who love
what she brings
unintentionally:

eternal life without her.

Cherry Lip Balm

The smoke tendrils around my wrists and ties down my
ankles,
pulls me in every direction until, one by one,
my joints begin to pop
like a candy powder on a child's tongue
in the heat of summer
outside that convenience store across from our house,
where we first kissed and I tasted your
cherry lip balm and your light beer.
My teeth begin to grate
and the shavings build up in my throat
until I choke back the tears
that have built up over years,
adulterated by the fears
of losing you to this cancer;
it's more than this little heart of mine can bear.

Who knew burning your photo
could be so dangerous?

The Urn

She sat at an old desk
made of oak,
writing old words
about an old lover
for whom she poured
the last pieces of her
tattered soul out
into the urn
in which
sat his
ashes.

The Liquor Store Grasshopper

11 p.m.

Every bloody night.

11 p.m.

So many writers talk about the early hours of the morning as a time where they feel the great weight of love sitting upon their chest like a demon Beelzebub sends out to rouse the God-fearing from a peaceful slumber,

but for me, it is 11 p.m.

11:01 p.m. was my Heaven; and anything before 10:59 p.m., my Hell.

It was always up until that last minute, when the willpower would fade and I would weasel my way out of the car and into the hen house to pluck the one or two eggs that would seal the evening for me and wrap it up with a beautiful wine-soaked bowtie. Because, you know, I was never the ant when it came to drinking; I wasn't one for stockpiling the shelves, reining in the harvest into beautifully built storehouses so that when famine set in, I'd be sitting pretty. I was the lazy grasshopper, waiting until the last minute to indulge the senses just one last time before sleep came and washed away my worries. But when the locusts came and went and left me there, sober, emaciated, and grey, standing but dead, I decided that I must wait just one more minute for 11:01 p.m. because that was when the liquor store closed and I would be free at least until morning.

Harvest

Reap in me the harvest
of a lifetime of loving someone
who could not love me back
with the same zeal and captivity as I.
Set fire to the vines
that bore bad fruit
and trim the excess
until all that's left to do
is admit
nothing is more painful
than coming back from a day
in the fields
and not having a
harvest home to come back to.
so please,
next time,
don't plant your seeds
of discontent in my heart.

My Sober Little Moon by: Jon Lupin, The Poetry Bandit

Worth

I crave a wakefulness
only grace can provide,
that won't let me go when the
tidal waves of self-doubt wash ashore;
I want this relentless awareness,
which is meant to wear me down,
make me ready to admit that

I am ready to live a life
worth celebrating.

Quiet Symphony

His addiction
was a noisy gong,
and her voice
was never loud enough.

Butterfly Whispers

Have you ever had a butterfly land on your shoulder and whisper, "everything is going to be alright"? Of course you haven't.

The truth is, before I walked into that meeting, my first AA meeting, this is what I wanted the most. I prayed so hard for God to send me that butterfly, to land it just so, and put those bloody words into its stupid little head. I just wanted not to go in there, not to meet those people, not to lay my heart on the table as a 7th tradition – I had forgotten to bring money. My uncle said it would be good for me; my dead uncle said it would be very good for me, but whether the uncles were dead or alive, I just didn't want to do this.

Just when I was about to turn away, a sweet old thing opened the door and invited me in.

"I didn't ask to be here," I said.

"That's not how it works," she replied.

And she was right. It's not. When nothing else in life works the way you want it to, you force it and you get exactly what you asked for, just not in the way that you expected.

She took me by the hand, even though I smelled like a dying man and brought me to the room. I sat down and she left me there without saying a word in a room full of people all living the same life as me, but just at a different speed. A few minutes later, I forgot all about that bloody butterfly and figured the uncles were right.

Wine, Worry, War Pt. 1

Every morning, I stand in front of the mirror and look at myself while I brush my teeth. I rarely smile at myself anymore, but once in a while, the reflection surprises me and I can barely believe that it was me that started it.

I stand sideways and look at my arms and pretend they are powerful enough to hold my children and weak enough to let them go, just far enough to the cliff's edge to make me feel like I'm doing a good job.

I see the tired skin beginning to build up where my hips should be; my underwear band is folding in half now and I blame the anxiety medication I was on, but deep down I know it's because I secretly hate myself. I hate that I can't get my ass out the door and exercise because I'm afraid. I'm always afraid. It's what I do.

Wine, worry, and war. They're always on my mind and I can't shake knowing that those three will always be sitting there with me, right around my midsection for as long as the four of us are alive.

I spit, rinse, and put my toothbrush back, clean the sink and then the mirror. Then the toilet and the shower, the floors and the walls and the next thing I know it's three hours later and I have nothing to show for the time but a clean house that no one really cares about, let alone me. I don't get swept away by the obsessiveness because I want to prove anything to anyone. Nothing about this is for show, but it's a way for me to escape the wine, worry, and wars that rage underneath this thick skin and it gets claustrophobic in there.

My sweet wife can see this now, and I am thankful for her touch and I hold her tight as the urge to continue to clean and clean and clean passes away. It has taken me a long time to learn this, but I have a fear of losing my grip on what has taken so long to embrace. God knew what he was doing when he knew it wouldn't be good for me to be alone.

My Sober Little Moon by: Jon Lupin. The Poetry Bandit

Master of Lies

I am the master of lies,
a mister of spies
administrator of dark skies,
the sinister minister
of a department of
boot lickers,
time bomb tickers,
and Pete's sake pickers.
So pack up your stickers,
playtime is over.
So pay the cover,
dance with your lover,
and bid me farewell,
because the truth
is all you needed and
for me to be sober.

Bile

Churning and burning, my stomach bites hard, reminding me there is something missing in the crop circles cut into my soul. The holes are large enough for my persona to pass through, into the vacuum left by bringing a scythe to my addiction to alcohol. That's probably what it was, and it feels okay for that to happen. I'm losing a part of myself that I loved, or at least thought I loved, and replacing it with something else. I don't know what that looks like yet, but I'll figure it out. In the meantime, it's time to plant some seeds in those holes and see what grows.

Detox

The back of my skull
opens up
and the tiny spiders emerge
and carry away the last of
my lust for the drink –
but why, oh why,
do they have to be so small
and so many?

Sobering Up

The heat sweats,
the cold shifts,
the fog lifts
and I begin to sift through
the ashes of the past week
searching for my dignity
only to find a note
scrawled hastily
telling me it has up and left.

Softly

Touch me softly
like you would a newborn,
for now I know
I am truly alive –
the sweat and
the Sweetness
tell me I am.

Fool's Gold

When you sit with broken people,
who just wish to make the hurting stop,
you realize, truly realize,
why faith in anything else or anyone
on this planet
is fool's gold.

Sad Wilderness

There's not much more you can do, is there?

I can see it.

There ... in the deserts where your eyes used to be. That kind of dryness only comes when a famine of emotion has invaded and left you with nothing but a noticeable absence from me.

You've cried your saline lifeline into the darkest of valleys, trying to fill them up, to create a liquid storehouse of lost dreams you can obsess over, and it's not hard to imagine that you'd build yourself a little cabin there, beside this lake of tears. I'm sure you'd run your fingers through the thick saltiness of the water and taste it upon the tip of your tongue, remembering times you used to feel them rolling down on your apple cheeks.

Hide as you may in this sad wilderness, but I will find you and when I do, I will drink from that lake, taste regret for myself, and try to understand you the best I can. So let's start there, together, and maybe we can bring some moisture back to the parched earth behind your eyes.

I Never Know

As I sip my coffee, now slightly colder than the last time you looked at me, I realize there are so many opportunities given to learn from our mistakes and how rarely we take them. So while I try to bring some light into the small, dark corner of this universe we like to call home, I ask how you are.

I never know what you'll say, or how you'll say it. I never know which woman will show up and love me today, but like a child banging on a tin can drum, I will sound my love for you. There is nothing that any of your beautiful sides could do to drive me away, and even though I hate cold coffee and I hate a cold shoulder, I will give you all the space you need and try again tomorrow, and tomorrow, and tomorrow until we figure this all out.

Leeches

I was never any good
at being good enough
for the
leeches who attached themselves
to my heart;
they always died a horrible death,
starving, as it were.

Killing Field

The snakes always wait in tall grass for
unsuspecting lovers to roll past.
They give a little bite on the heel,
some poison to feel the
inevitable heartache that
comes in the morning,
because real love
is never found in the meadow.
It is only shot, skinned, cleaned,
and fried over the fires of Hell,
then consumed by those not fit for
eating with the living.
So make your love while you can,
because you have until sunrise
to realize that the place in which you lie
is the killing field
for lovers' sighs.

The Four Corners of My Life

These were my Four Horsemen who came to me with great fury in the later years of my life, when my faith was its weakest and I had been dealt a blight:

1. Alcoholism – He is the Convincer. With honey on his tongue and a serpent in his pocket, he rides in from the south bringing comfort at first and then death at the end.
2. Anxiety – She wears a dress that leaves nothing to the imagination, for she is afraid of judgement, but passes it over the people as if it were a blessing to them. She is with child for eternity and suffers the pain of childbirth every day without result. She has named him Worry.
3. Obsession – His helm and armor is dark and if you would search for his eyes… he has none. He is blind to everything around him; he cares not for the weak or for the injured. He speaks rarely, but if he does, his voice carries on until you forget what your own sounds like.
4. Guilt – His presence is commanding, even though he is but a shadow that needs no light to live. Him, I fear most, for he carries the broadest of swords and does so with ease, and with it he leads the others in battle.

It was clear to me that they would all fall one day and my Will would finally live without fear, and it was with this Hope that I held my ground, and still battle them to this day.

O Quivering Lip

O Quivering Lip,
must you be?
If there was a planet I could color for you,
it would have rings –
something for you to put on each of your
elegant and slender fingers.
If there was a great cedar that
I could climb and retrieve a branch
meant only for doves
after the floods
for all the spilled blood,
I would and
I would bring it to you
to show you there is always life
after war.
O Quivering Lip,
can't you see?
I would do anything for thee.

Eve

I joined a defeated dirge,
lead-footed and lacking hope,
as a has-been hack of a man,
making mysterious music,
singing that
I could save myself.
And while I danced,
she came to me,
a slave to a ballet
that kept her heart
infinitely dancing to
a song of deliverance,
a song that
melted from her tongue,
dripping off her lips and
onto my dry skin which was
cracked and worn from
wondering if relief had finally come
in the form of a woman.

The Sweetness

While Grief mocked me
where I lay,
and Anger skipped through the
puddles of my secrets
spilled upon the barroom floor,
I was reminded why I shouldn't
drink with strangers,
and
I was reminded
I hadn't changed,
despite my promises.

So with a "hey-nonny-nonny"
and a "hip-hip-hurrah,"
I picked myself up
and called it a draw;
neither Grief
nor the Anger
would follow me home,
for I called up the Sweetness
and told her the truth:
I wanted to change
before I lost all my youth.
She nodded and sighed
and took me back in
and I'll never forget it
as long as I live.

My Sober Little Moon by: Jon Lupin, The Poetry Bandit

Dinner Guests

When I'm with her,
even my demons
dress up for dinner
and behave.

Shells

Shells. We all have one and we all decide how big to make it as we grow up. We pass judgement on what to let in and what to leave out. Our whole lives are lived in that shell, and whether it is spacious or cramped, we expect that everyone else respects that shell and stays the hell out of it if they didn't make the cut. I think the kind of man I want to be now is one who doesn't have a shell, because what I have learned is the more time I spend creating a perfect little world inside that shell, the fewer chances I will have to help others. Yeah, we all have our shells, but more often than not, I see a few of us on our backs, squirming and kicking and screaming, trying to aright ourselves. The answer isn't found inside the shell, but I think it can be found in helping others understand that they don't need one. Surround yourself with the right people, and you won't need one either.

Burdens

Be vulnerable in the most precious of ways;
let us see
your yoke is heavy,
dripping in sludge,
creeping with sins,
bathing in an unholy mist,
because that smile isn't fooling anyone,
least of all you.
I can see it in the lines that crease
the skin around the crying fields
of your sweet face that
you planted seeds of discontent in
last season,
and now,
you wait for sadness to grow.
You say you enjoy the waiting,
and when it is time to reap,
you enjoy that as well,
including everything the next season
promises
when planting
your lowered expectations.
But at least share the yoke,
because a burden isn't ugly
when shared with someone who cares.

Tiny Birds

Your tiny birds
built a nest
inside the cavity
I carved out
especially for you.

Time Is a Man Eater

There's a clock ticking in this house in quite the carnivorous way; it eats away at my nicely tanned skin, exposing the bones and parts of my interior that I hide from your eyes. It steals the time I need to deal with the parts of my old nature that keep me from moving forward. I have to find this clock. I must! If I do not stop it from ticking the tocks and smoothing the rocks in the river that sweeps over the valleys in my chest, I'm afraid that I'll be forever stuck in that instant. But maybe I'm being dramatic again. It's not like I can do anything about it, because even if I do find it and pull out its guts, spring by spring, prying the pendulum from its perch, where it hypnotizes the handsome sins to stay for another round, I'm bound to hear another clock, somewhere in my house or even worse, inside my body. Then again, maybe that's why I feel time eats away at the best parts of me – maybe there's something inside time wants me to see, something that will make all the waiting and the drama worth it.

My Sober Little Moon by: Jon Lupin, The Poetry Bandit

F o x h o l e

Hold my hand,
just as you did
on the day that I left
to become a man.

I returned in shackles,
no one sees the pain
as the jackals
defile my name.

You see me as I am,
scares the beaver from the dam,
I retreat all alone;
safety is found inside the foxhole.

I am content sometimes
to let my body groove
into the sticks and stones and
the feathers of this natural deathbed.

But like a tree, I will fall
and make a sound
that will shake the feet
of these Hallowed Halls.

You see me as I am,
scares the beaver from the dam,
I retreat all alone;
safety is found inside my foxhole.

It's Bright Where You Are

Working like clockwork
for so long now,
it's habit
but when the schedule is broken,
punch a hole in my token,
because I have to get out of here;
it's bright where you are.

Monotony and autonomy,
snipers, watching me like a criminal,
but I love being punctual,
so I play the role,
but I have to get out of here;
it's bright where you are.

And I see love does much more
than trivialize and ritualize
the motives and motions
we rehearse for the moment,
because I have to get out here;
it's bright where you are.

Working like clockwork
for so long now,
it's habit.

Idle Factory

I imagine that our hearts are somewhat like
idle factories,
waiting for items or monuments to receive
in the shipping bay,
beginning a process of fawning
and molding,
casting its clay around the object of desire.
Then when all the engineering is complete,
the production machine in the
chamber to the top left kicks into high gear
and begins to replicate,
animate, and create
whatever it is that it desires most,
and when the mind has no interest
in the product,
it will mothball that factory until the
eyes spy
the next little lie
to latch on to and
commit idolatry with.

DMZ

Walking through your shadow
was like taking a stroll
through the fields of
wild poppies and
buried bombs.

Work of Fiction

Behind our bedroom walls,
we are a work of fiction,
a story told late at night to
frighten young children
from dreaming of the
happily never ever
after we drank that warm milk
to drown the burning feelings
which don't sit well.

So I ask you,
what story do we tell our children,
instead of this slanted
rusted version of
their wildest dreams of
two people getting along?
Is it possible that the
same lessons they learn
and what we learned on the
same merry-go-rounds
are just too hard to understand?

Something was missing and still is.

Reptilian

I think people are much like reptiles in the way we both
shed our skins. We grow and we grow, and the outer
layers feel tight, birthing this feeling of claustrophobia
inside our own bodies, and the easiest thing to do is either
buy new clothes and suffer inside stretched skin, or we can
burn those epidermal badlands and grow something new.

I was told as a boy that every human has two natures: one
new and one old, existing together, battling and jostling for
position within our hearts. I didn't understand what this
meant then, but I do now as I sit here in my office and
watch my Tiger Salamander, Stripes, wriggle and writhe
himself out of a sloppy, dirty membrane.

I think it's about time I joined him, but the question that I
can't seem to answer is what will happen to my skin once I
have shed it? Will it sit in my basement or under my bed, in
case I get homesick? Will I save it for a rainy day, when I'm
home alone and no one is watching? Will I truly be able to
burn it for good, or will I burn it for money? I don't know,
but what I do know is that Stripes will shed that skin until
he dies, and just maybe so will I.

(update: Stripes died 2 months before this book was published)

The Third Law

There was something so
beautiful and familiar
in the way we fell apart;
it was like we were built with
second-hand parts and
were destined to
repeat our
mistakes.

What It Was Like

I've reheated my coffee about three times now, I think –
could be more actually, but in this haze of indecisiveness
I've lost count. It's all I have lately, the coffee. I lost my
chance at drinking like a normie, squandered it like a ten-
year-old wastes five bucks in quarters at the arcade in a
single sitting of "Fantasy Sword." There are days when I
look at the oil rainbows in that caffeinated sludge and think
about all the times when I should have had just one glass
or one beer. But I know, with me, there is no such thing as
"just one" – the very idea is as preposterous as stating the
earth is flatter than Satan's ironing board. So "just one"
was always "just a bottle" or "just one more", and there's
no justifying it. It's a terrible thing to sit back and think
coffee isn't good enough, because it has to be, for me. I've
ruined my chance to be normal.

I have to remember I have a drawer in my dresser full of
clothes I've ruined with wine over the years, but I don't
have a single piece of clothing stained with coffee, so I
guess that's something.

Acid Wash

There were days
when the rain was more like an acid wash
as I sat outside
waiting for you to return to yourself;
I always went outside to kill time,
though it usually felt
like I was killing myself,
heaping the blame
into the furnace like
coal in a locomotive stomach,
white-hot and without ceasing.
But I learned
even though the fire grew
to Babylonian measures,
my love was always standing there
like four friends,
stronger in the flame
but unconsumed.
So while I sat there,
outside and enkindled in a
pity party thrown for one,
it was always easy to remember
the fire never
singed my simple love for you.

Reparations

Piling and complied,
folded neatly,
pristine and undefiled,
stood this little mound
outside my bedroom door.
It consisted of all the compliments
you took from me,
never paid back in full.
I took that personally,
and put it next to
addiction and obsession,
these two runaways I had picked up
from the corner store when I was 20.
Nevertheless,
the mound grew, because I let it,
and even though it was difficult to
get around,
get away,
get real,
get things done,
I always came back to the fact
I was shallow enough
to fold my dirty laundry
and expect you to
put it away.
I was so foolish,
but from now on,
I'll clean up after myself.

Blake's Lamb

You had a little lamb
and its heart was pure as snow,
but it found that little box
under your bed.
Now we stroll and patrol
these streets full of wolves
and rolled up sleeves,
hoping that maybe
we'll find a lamb,
still,
instead of a tiger
burning hot under the
apricot lamp light,
caught between a home
and a hard place.

My Sober Little Moon by: Jon Lupin, The Poetry Bandit

Mocking Moon

Tonight, the moon is full of itself,
glowing brightly upon us,
mocking us.
Tomorrow will soon be here,
its soft velvet grip slowly curling
around our throats, and
we have nothing to show for today,
except a few tears and cold cups of coffee.
But we could stand here
and allow this hypnotic
lunar fitness to hold us,
or we can dust off
our bag of bones and polish up
the dancing shoes,
because tonight, my dear,
seems a perfect night to do some haunting.

My Sober Little Moon by: Jon Lupin, The Poetry Bandit

My Sober Little Moon by: Jon Lupin, The Poetry Bandit

Verbal Entity

We had difficulties
speaking emotions into
verbal entities,
so you asked me for a letter,
but I refused,
for everything you had to know
was written in the
aging lines of my face.

Sweet Oblivion

At dawn,
the fingers of daylight find their way
to a land of unfinished pleasures,
of yellow brick roads
abandoned by lesser men,
of endless poppy fields
waiting to be written into
lore and wars fought
by mechanized mantras.

It is in those moments
that I will lose myself
in your sweet oblivion.

Relapse

Tonight ends a short run at being sober. I feel that I may be doomed as a human, so I think of whatever else it is that I could do in this damaged state and be excellent at it. It hits me that we may have a free will, may not be perfect and may have been well-meaning people in the past. It's possible, I mean, if you check the historical texts, there's not a lot of information about angels leaving me with a small window to fit through. I could break my way out of this human skin and wind up with wings one day. Yeah. I could be a decent angel. I think I could be very good at helping other drunken poets figure out where the line needs to be drawn, but knowing me, I'd draw it in the sand – easily erased or moved or disguised by the rising tides of uneasiness and low self-esteem. So maybe I should stick to what I know: second chances. I'll get it right, one day at a time.

(Written immediately after a week of relapse in early 2015)

Workin' Stiffs

We're just a couple of hard working folks,
working on us,
working on filling the cracks in our age-old embraces
with whatever time we have left
in our own souls;
even then, we are always thinking about the other,
because we both sin,
we have our flaws.
It is what makes us
aware of what little time we have left
to make our mark.

In the Annex

Steal away, my precious,
to a place where we can be
delicious and repetitious,
sacrifice the duplicitous
and embrace the religious
until everyone who must walk past
does so with plugs
in their devious little ears.

Tired Stones

This background battlefield
is set in parasitic solitude,
my incessant groans for
attention harvested and
blown away into the wind,
chaff-like,
swept in to the corners of
empty harvest homes;
dead moss on tired stones,
nothing left to drink
but what I have sown.

Cut Teeth

We all have cut our teeth on bad calls and hid our faults from the ones who love us too much, without prejudice. It gives us a thick hide, a patchwork of tough skin and matted fur, and we wear it like a uniform, proud to be a member of an army of people now walking as animals. We wake up afraid for being accosted and go to sleep with that third eye open, waiting for someone we love to stab us in the back. So the hide never comes off, but it gets heavier with each day, with each passing moment, gets thicker, water logged with our own tears and sweat. It can be a chore just to breathe under the ballasts of this ponderous pressure we created for ourselves, but we remind ourselves that this is a uniform and we are at war, albeit with a force completely of our own creation. We know that it's better to play the victim and sharpen our fictitious fangs on the flesh of fallacies only we know about. So, under the weight of our own lies we'll pretend we're still hunted and haunted, and hope to high water that the ones we love and love us back never figure it out.

Forgiving

I am afraid,
bone-shakingly frightened,
the damned have risen
from their acute slumber
behind desks and stations,
from behind veils and untorn curtains,
and have come to worship
at my feet
asking for second chances.
I'm afraid
I can't do anything but listen
to their derision and dissolution
and delusional demands of me
and of people
I don't even know.
What good am I when
I am no better than they?

Why is that I always fade
like a fire in winter
when someone asks me
for forgiveness?

Hope and Prayer

There's a Peacefulness that I miss in my life, and I long for it to return. I do, however, catch glimpses of it still, holding hands with Hope, and a Prayer lingers behind them as a playful only-child does with his imaginary friends. I wait for them to skip my way, lay out their picnic blanket and invite me to join… but it never happens; either I keep retreating from them or they are frozen in time, never nearing me but always pretending to. I feel like I'm in a terrible dream from which I might awake drunk, ashamed and waiting desperately for that peacefulness to come back and save me.

Wax and Wane

We had the kind of souls
that waxed in the evening and
waned in daylight.
It was never easy to distinguish between
light and the dark when we were in a
room together, and maybe that is why
it was so difficult for us to see what was
really happening to us.
We were so focused on surviving the day
inattention to the little things
was what was driving the tent pegs
deeper and deeper into our temples;
things like a lack of sweat in the shower,
smiles over brushing our teeth in the morning,
singing a favorite tune with a look and a peck on the
cheek,
or a light brushing of your hair from your forehead so I
could
caress it with mine.
I'm tired of surviving the day, my love;
let's say we try living for the night again?

Couch Sleeping

After days like today,
you like to sleep on the couch,
your breath hard yet free
from the nightmare of having
to hold it all day long,
yet again.
I want to wake you,
bring you to bed,
tuck you in,
kiss your forehead,
fast forward tomorrow,
so that you can be here again,
breathing freely in your sleep,
on our couch,
in our house,
safe
for the moment
from your mind.

My Sober Little Moon by: Jon Lupin, The Poetry Bandit

Build a Better Man

My wife once told me that
skin is thin,
like paper.
A tear, a drop of blood,
something memorable
makes a stain upon the skin,
changing it;
it's no longer innocent or
sheen, or
clean, or
righteous in its invitation
to experience art or
love or
true love.
I think of skinned knees
on my children,
how each one is a
taste of learning.
I think of each bruise and cut
I received working
on myself,
building a better man.
And then I think of her,
how I just want to
wrap her back up
in that protective plastic
the newspaper comes in.
I don't want her skin
touched by the pen of the world,
but she assures me
even though
it's too late for that,
she will be alright.
Her skin is not like mine;
"It's thicker," she says with a smile.

My Sober Little Moon by: Jon Lupin, The Poetry Bandit

The Memorial

I couldn't recall when it became
a problem, this hanging onto the idea
of everything having a place, a home.
I do, however,
have a specific memory of when
I was eight years old, of walking home from school,
scouring the ground
for the lost things
from other people's lives,
thinking there has to be
a happy ending for this,
this thing I just picked up.
To me,
there was something sad
about people tossing things away,
because it meant they did not make
an effort to find it a place.
I called them "lost memories."
I would take them home,
hang them on my wall with a tack and
soon my little 8 x 8 room became a
memorial to the part of the
human spirit I began to despise the most.
And today, I feel cemeteries are much like my wall
of lost things,
gravestones tossed on the ground
only visible for the first visit,
then forgotten.
"Oh, we have the memory, son."
Do we?
If we have nothing to prompt us
to remember the person in the first place,
what's the point?
I don't think we love people
the way we used to,
and that leaves me sad,
like an eight year old boy
picking up another wedding ring
on his way home from school.

Riot

We were a riot on fire,
rolling through the streets
of a city without a king,
waiting for our time
where our voices could
stand in the squares
without pistols
as witness
to our
illness.

Mercy Kill

I walked into the room
with a song in my head
and a promise on my tongue,
but it was clear to me
the look in your eye
was begging for me
to move on,
check out,
forgive and forget
and to let you go.
All this and more
you wanted to give me
as a mercy kill,
something you
dreamed up on your darkest day.
I made a promise
and it doesn't matter
how bad it gets
or what kind of burden
you think you might be
adding to my yoke.
You could release
Hell's hounds,
the juggernaut jerks,
flicker-eyed fellows and
the bear hunter,
I will never leave you,
because
I know,
the depression will pass
and a maniac moment
will send us careening
into a tear soaked reverie,
a prayer that will not
dare to end for days.

Before...

When I hug your waist and
put my ear upon your abdomen,
there is a cacophony of sound
I have to sort through.
I have to strain my ears,
clear my mind and
listen carefully for the laughter.
I know it's there and
you do, as well.
I know you've buried it deep in there,
amongst the two empty cribs
and the three full beds, but
it's not their laughter I'm looking for –
it's yours.
You know,
that laughter you dispersed like candy
on All Hallows' Eve
when you were younger,
before you knew real pain,
before you learned how to drive,
before you made your first dollar,
before you had your first child,
before you lost your first child.
I will find that laughter again,
and when I do, I will record it.
I will play it for you every day
when you wake up,
because I believe that
anyone who hears
their own laughter again
will feel as if they've heard
a symphony,
a work of art
that will change
their day for the better.

Live it

Slowly but surely,
I will chew away this
pathetic excuse of an exterior.
The ground around me
will be littered with the
old pieces of me
I dared not swallow;
all that will be left
is the life
you begged me
to live,
and I will live it.

Plundering

When the stars are
rent asunder
and the heart breaks -
the sound of thunder -
I will bury the blunders
six feet under
all by myself
because I alone
did the plundering
of what once was
my childlike wonder.

The Convincer

All men try,
pray and pry at the
treasure chest filled with
rich opportunities to make
a name for themselves,
while I'm over here,
licking the universe's boots,
turning my faith
into a cage,
full of rage and heat.
I'm never sure when to stop,
so I just keep going,
pour another glass,
and I just keep going.
"It's the way of the world," I say,
trying to convince myself
the book on the shelf
with the busted spine
isn't mine.
"Just one vice for me
in this life," I say,
hoping no one
heard me,
but it's so easy to be right
when you are
talking to yourself.

Jazz Piano

I forgot how much I love jazz piano; it takes only a moment of listening to it to take me away from the mosh pit in my head. Minors and majors, all bouncing around in a cacophony, organized in such a way that I feel like chaos has an order. When you suffer from obsessive thoughts and Obsessive Compulsive Disorder, as I do, you tend to crave symmetry and straight edges, geometry and long ledges, schedules and unbroken pledges. I immerse myself in a tempo that's systematic, and I cling to it. I need that plan, which I stayed up till 2:37 a.m. writing on sheet music with pen, to be without error and I need it to unfold in a similar fashion. So when I start the day and it does not go according to plan, all hell is unleashed in my mind and I find it very hard to recover the day. "Pray," "Trust," "Faith," are thrown at me like rice on a wedding day, but it doesn't help. Medication didn't help. But jazz piano. Jazz piano reminds me though a song can start off in discord, if you let it, the unpredictability becomes an adventure and it always ends so sweetly, like the soft hands of my daughters on my rough, creasing face, like my son's rare expression of love for "just being a great dad," and as sweetly as the soft fingers of my poetess, calming the agitation in my skull.

Jazz piano, order found in chaos.

OCD

I've left that memory on the floor now
for over a week. The urge to give in to
OCD and mop it up or sweep it under a rug
is so strong, but I want to prove to you,
and to myself, that I can leave it there.
It helps me stay sane (in your terms and
understanding though), and it helps.
I struggle to keep it together most days, but only
do so by dusting and wiping old names away,
cleaning out closets,
rearranging my stories and lies, and believing
one day I can clean up that memory
without hating myself for doing so.

Wine, Worry, War Pt.2

When I awake, Wine, Worry, War,
sit with leashes in their mouths,
waiting for the morning walk.
I've barely time to wipe sleep's
mischief from my eyes
and already they want my
attention.
And I give it. I have to.
They are always on my mind,
I'm enslaved.
Certain parts of my mind
don't fire the right kind of weapons
to fight off their reminders.
For example,
I could be arranging
my life in alphabetical order
and War will remind me that it needs
to be groomed,
or Wine will bark, and bark, and bark,
and bark and never stop,
until I give it what it wants.
Worry is different.
She just follows me around,
somewhat like that mangy mutt,
Guilt does from time to time.
I didn't have any pets until
I started to live sober,
and I'm hoping that one day
I can have real dogs.
For now, Wine, Worry, and War
will have to do.

No Longer Caged

Why is the soul caged, entrapped by a sloppy skin of sin, stuck in something as clairvoyant as the fogged up window at a drive-in movie? You know that feeling you get, when the adrenaline is pumping, the hair stands up on end and it flows from the back of your neck behind the ears and races down your spine, then down your arms, and fills your hands with swollen urge to throw them up in the air and scream? That's not adrenaline, my friend. That's your soul trying to get out of this sticky situation of a body. It's a pure form of excitement our Higher Power planted in each of us before we were even born. Those goosebumps: millions of hands, tiny fingers pushing, trying to stretch for the first time in centuries.

We all feel it. To deny that we're more than flesh and bone, blood and failure, would be the ultimate definition of laziness. One day, we'll break out of this flawed mold and we will be free, no longer moving in slow motion, no longer caged.

Dumpster Fire

Take it down to the
border town and douse it in gasoline,
light a match and walk away for a quick
recap of my plausible deniability.
Where was I?
What was I doing?
Who was I drinking with?
Was that four? Five? Ten?
Her trust disappeared into the Blood Alley
for a glass of dumpster wine and slight of
homeless hand, followed with a black out
date with Fate, Despair and that witch, Guilt.
So where was I when I lit this
life on fire, anyway?
I don't recall,
but I'm sure whatever this addict has to say
won't hold up in your court of
lawlessness anyway.

For the Masses

You once told me that it was natural,
and that it was alright to feel as if
someone had plucked your soul from your
screaming and fatigued flesh,
like a kitten needing saving from being in a
basket for Cleopatra to find.
I don't feel like I've been saved;
I don't feel as if this sack of bones is better off
without my soul,
or maybe,
that's the point.
Maybe I had to be reminded
there's nothing here for me anymore,
nothing worth crying about,
nothing meaningful to argue over,
nothing but brittle people
boasting over skin that is tired of
cellphone flashes and magazine lies,
selfie caches and collagen cries;
there's nothing left for us to
make our own
except that which doesn't belong here:
The soul is your own
so stop selling it to the masses.

Once

I once was a lost cause,
like Satan
in a white robe.

Sober Soul

O, Sober soul,
why do you mock yourself so?
You can't see this forest for the trees yet,
but you will;
these majestic cedars and towering pines,
these evergreen glens and fern palaces –
they all belong to you
and your hungry, hungry heart.

Prison Break

When I release myself
from the prison
between my ears,
I will collect my things,
step into the light,
and recall that life is better lived
out here
with beautiful people
like you.

Poor Bugger

Waning moonlight is my
favorite kind
because it hides this skin,
pale and stretched
over bones
set like tent poles after
strong winds,
housing a precarious soul,
always carrying a spade or two
still dirty from the last poet
I buried under a pile
of his own words;
and it never makes me happy
and that's okay.
I stopped believing anything
would bring me that.
So I will pull this thin skin
tighter,
hugging this bag of sober trouble,
and wait for the next
poor bugger
to show me his heart.

34,056

Yesterday,
you touched the back
of my neck
and said, "I love you"
for the 34,056th time,
but to me,
it will always feel like
the first.

Absence

The absence of love
has the same colour
as my shadow,
and though my shadow
has always been
colour blind
even it knows
when it's time
to abandon the darkness
and step into the light.

Hiatus

She took a hiatus
from being the perfect lady,
and from the notion
she was here to please
everyone else;

in the leaving
she was born again.

Don't Do It

If, and not when, you feel there is nothing left to do but look at what is on the other side of that door (you know, the one you can never open or close again), remember there is always someone out here who cannot live without you. So talk to them, even if you don't know who they are yet, because it will surprise you how many will listen to you and how many will say they love you.

Post Acute Withdrawals

I'm a mess.
My eyes are blotchy,
my skin is numb,
there is a ringing in my ears that will
not be quiet,
and though it reminds me
I'm still alive,
I keep asking myself
"Why?" and,
"How long?"
"How long will this last?
How long until the demolition derby
in my mind ends
with just one thought standing?
And what thought will that be?
Will it be the one that does me in?
Will it be the one that saves me?"
No one knows the answer to these
questions but me
and the Great Inbetween.

OCD, Part 2

I have to admit, I never saw any of this becoming part of my reality; to know that my fear and worry has finally found a period instead of a comma, well, that is like Manna, my friends, bread from heaven to soak in oil instead of tears, like a last meal on your last day but knowing that the hangman isn't coming because his grandmother passed away from natural causes, and he isn't coming back because she left him a lot of money and a boat to sail around the Caribbean in. Freedom, of some sort, is what I have realized that I am afforded now because of some tiny little orange pill which I must take with food, each morning, with half a glass of orange juice, at exactly 7:34am after I eat a bowl of fiber-rich cereal in a cup of almond milk, and not before or after, because if I take it later I get really tired at 1:13pm. But this, my friends, is more beautiful to me than any eclipse of a moon, a sun or a heart.

I have OCD and I take a medication to manage it, and I'm pretty damn proud of that.

Chained

Since I can remember
I have been fighting against the life
I never wanted.
It kept me from getting close
to a feeling I could trust.
Then,
when I was chained to a wall,
you came and offered me a key.
Sometimes the key
fits the lock on the
manacles, and sometimes
it doesn't.
I hope one day
that it will fit
all the time
because I see freedom
in loving you.

Duress

Duress is the dress code when you are left for dead,
before crossing the threshold. It looked good on you. Isn't
that what you wanted? To be first through the door with a
"come hither and wither at the feet of my story" kind of look
down your nose at the rest of the demons who just showed
up to play cards or bridge or some other game requiring
only talons and bad luck? Maybe that's what I couldn't
stand about you; always first through the pew, always last
in the line, checking out the stitches in the britches of other
guys' bitches; never shy to the eye, always long in the
throat and never a moat wide enough to keep the whores
and the gamers at bay.

You loved it, and that's why you went out with a bang,
pupils maxed out, not a drop of sweat left to spare the
Reaper when he came to bind you up in a three piece suit.

Duress was the dress code, and it looked good on you,
too good.

Birthday Cards

I kept all my birthday cards after I turned 35.
Because when I turned 35, that is when the
world finally felt real to me;
when the pain of losing life which was
part you, part me, but all angel,
twice;
when the pain of realizing the damage done
with drinking had delivered a killing blow,
leaving me lying on the floor of a
slaughterhouse Life had only used for
sad sacks of flesh;
when the world had finally grown tired of my stories
and I felt there was only one tale left to tell,
no one stuck around to listen …
no one, that is, but you.

So that is why I keep my birthday cards now,
to remind me when life was difficult,
that I'm still here by the grace of God,
who I sometimes have a hard time mustering
a capital "G" for, but continue to
trust will allow me to collect these cards from
the persons who love me best.

The First Time Going to the Supermarket Sober

After paying for the groceries you sent me out for, I sat in my car for about thirty minutes, listening to a shitty song that makes me cry every time; I don't know why, but that's not what's bothering me as I open up the party size bag of chocolate covered peanuts I bought just for me, to eat, alone, in my sadness. It seemed like a good idea in the store, and it was an even better idea when I started to feel the rush of sugar slowly careen around inside my veins. So, looking over at the grocery store, there was the cashier who helped me, smoking a cigarette with her chubby little hand, gauntleted with an array of cheap rings she surely received as parting gifts from the men she swept up while cleaning the aisles late at night. She was crying, going on about something to a co-worker, batting away the tears with the back of her nicotine hands. I wanted to console her, tell her that whatever was wrong would seem insignificant compared to another sunrise … but she was smoking, and I hated the smell of cigarette smoke, and most importantly, I didn't want to share the sadness of my moment. I wanted all the sadness to myself.

I felt sick to my stomach as the song and the party bag of chocolate covered peanuts finished up. She put out her cigarette and went back inside, receiving half-assed consolation from her co-worker.

The bag was empty.
I was empty.

I really wanted to hug her.
I did.
Honest.

Weeping Willows

Weep for me,
as I fade in and out
of your sentences
like the setting sunlight
through branches of the
weeping willows
growing by the river banks
where we once swam
on a hot summer's day,
like two sweaty beasts
in the light of love,
seeking vengeance against
a life lived prior without each other.

How could we have spent
so much time not even knowing
the other existed?
Thankful for the building up
of an intense desire to kiss you
during all these years
I allowed the willows to weep
as we devoured each other
all summer long.

Bad Breath

So, alone was how it had to be.
There could be only this survival,
written in the last pages of my life.
Bleak and stark,
they seemed to me, before the
makeshift deathbed
was turned down by the
maids of Hell –
at least they left a mint on the pillow
this time.
I would find out later
as I breathed my last
that it wasn't for me
but for him;
spending an eternity
in the Pit
makes for some
damn bad breath.

Chapel

I have learned
not to fight the voices
in my head.
So, I built a chapel
and made them my choir.

Hiding

Caught in the crosshairs
of embattled old souls
and young hearts,
burned scrolls and
poisoned words,
we hid
in our foxhole
until we could write
once more with that
love for language
on the tips of our tongues
dipped in the fiery ink
of a Leviathan
slain by the harpoons of
our clergyman's ire.

Soft

Soft,
is what she was,
never rough,
never coarse;
she sung sweetly,
never hoarse.
Power like energy,
real as matter,
pure at the source –
dangerous.
This is how I felt:
never safe,
never solid,
never sane,
always rabid;
giving in to addiction,
a beautiful habit.

Soft,
that is what she was.

My First Time Running into Someone from Recovery in Public

I spoke to her as if I knew
what it meant to have lost something
that was needed in a time of great peril.
She scoffed inside her heart,
it was apparent in the way she looked at her shoes
as I tried to reach out with words.
I was only doing what was taught to me
at a young age: empathy.
It is probably the most difficult thing
the human race must attempt on a daily basis
with the most devastating of consequences
when done incorrectly.
So while I left her in the frozen breakfast aisle
looking at hash browns,
I went home to find a new way
to thaw my good intentions.

Excavating

The truth is found in my
excavated chest,
behind the fossilized suicide of
heart and muscle and those
three little butterflies I kept below,
as in an ancient burial ground -
because we all know,
if you make something ancient
no one is allowed to disturb that area.
So that is where it will stay
until you breathe life,
breathe love,
breathe pity or gasps full of mercy
into my iron lungs.

I can only imagine how colourful those
three little butterflies will be
when you find them and
sigh upon them with your
steadfast love.

Come Back to Me

Come back to me
when you have nothing left,
because right now I can see
you holding on to that
shred of what you name "pride,"
but I call it "ego,"
or they'd call it "bravery."
We're not brave,
but you are holding on to this
notion you are in some way just like
everyone else – just another person
on this planet blessed with the ability
to do this in moderation.

Such a thing does not exist.

It is and ever will be
engraved upon the tombstones
up one side and right down the other
of this long road home.

When you get there,
give it up. All of it,
all this bullshit that says you need
a glimpse of heaven bathed in booze
in order to wash yourself clean
in the sweet light of recognition.

Come back to me,
but come back when you have
nothing left but
the will to live a new life,
one free of your old self.

Unraveled

I feel like I need a
good unraveling
right before my own eyes,
just so I can see
what fails,
what survives,
and what is destined for the fire.

What fails, I will set aside
to remind myself of what didn't work.
What survives, I will scrutinize and ask,
"Why did you make it and not the others?"
What is destined for the flame
I will not give a second thought to
other than the stench it emits
when it burns.

Courage

Courage, Dear Heart.
We have had our book
burned before,
and each time we write it over
it keeps getting better
and better.

Awaken

I want an awakening that
will excite these bones
for an eternity,
not just for a moment or two.
I want not to want, or need,
I'd simply like to be or to be here
or to be anywhere than stuck between
the ears or in the middle of those
wasted years getting wasted
or drying up in dry drunkenness.

I think I can get there,
because you're awake.
You have risen from a slumber
that stole five years, five years of
sad angry happiness which always seemed
to fade before I could find a way
for us to hold on to it.
That was then,
and this …
this is what it feels like to be Now,
and know it.
And know it.

Gold Rush

This residue
of love,
cast in clay-like shoes,
worn till broken
with no apology spoken,
between maddening
open mouth kisses
and fumbling hand misses,
you wore that
"I want you"
and I gave it all
only to be
sold down a river
panned for gold
by lesser men than I.

B & W

At some point
you need to understand
I will always be a
black sheep,
and I cannot be
painted white.

Weeping War

My tears
never dry up.
They run in trenches
like men with no names
in fields that once were green,
refusing to die,
alone and forgotten
or without having served
a purpose
other than the target practice
of a foe who has no love
for the men
who wish only
for dry cheeks in summer.

Like a Feather

Chaos has no weight
if there is
no restoration
afterwards.

The Store

The Light in your eyes
flickers like an old
halogen bulb in a convenience store
selling anything but that.
It has also run out of everything
you need to live a full life.
You wonder why you even walked in there?
If the only thing
you realize is that the
bulb needs changing,
you're on the right track.

Alcoholism

Alcoholism stole the parts of my adult life
I wish I could have said goodbye to,
because you see,
when you don't suffer from an addiction
you get a brief moment with yourself,
as you were, in the very instances that define you.
When you are being led away
from your future as you hoped it would be,
you do not get to say goodbye.
You do not get to make peace.
You do not get to give those loved ones
their last kiss …
at least not until you embrace
that ugliness,
name it,
and move forward, pressing on,
in the hope that every moment made
from then on
will make up for those you lost.

Spin the Bottle

Left foot,
right foot,
right on time,
and left for dead
on the cold steps of a temple
that had burned
a hole through our hearts
by the time we grew up.

So many rules for the body
and not enough for the heart,
and so I spin the wheel
one last time
to find out where I end up.

Parting Words

Don't give up on yourself;
you're still in there,
somewhere.

My Sober Little Moon by: Jon Lupin, The Poetry Bandit

About the Author:

Jon Lupin is a Canadian Poet, residing on the West Coast, and is a dedicated husband, father and writer. He has overcome an addiction to alcohol, a disease which he defeats daily with the help of his Higher Power and a community dedicated to helping alcoholics recover. In addition to this struggle he is a vocal advocate for ending the stigma surrounding mental illness as he also has been diagnosed with severe OCD/Pure OT. With this book, it is his hope that anyone struggling with drugs or alcohol, a difficult time in their lives, pain, loss or suffering can realize there is hope, there is a way out and a meaningful life can still be lived and enjoyed!

Contact or follow Jon:

Facebook | facebook.com/Jon Lupin as The Poetry Bandit
Twitter | twitter.com/thepoetrybandit
Tumblr | therealpoetrybandit.tumblr.com
Instagram | instagram.com/the_poetrybandit
Email | thepoetrybandit@gmail.com
Etsy | www.etsy.com/shop/thepoetrybandit

Made in the USA
Columbia, SC
16 September 2019